Pursuit of Happiness

by

James Peppe

PepTalks Media • Houston, Texas

Table of Contents

Preface

Sometimes the hardest things to see are the things directly in front of us.

Having suffered a traumatic childhood eye injury, I know how frustrating it can be when others point toward something that appears perfectly obvious to them while you struggle to bring it into focus yourself.

"It's right *there.*"

But impaired vision is not dishonesty.
It is not stupidity.
And it is certainly not a sign of moral failure.

Often, it simply means the picture itself is just too blurry, too distorted, or too cluttered to process clearly.

I have come to believe much of modern political life functions the same way.

Like Thomas Paine in 1776, most Americans know that things are terribly off track — that we simply cannot go on this way. They feel the frustration. They feel the exhaustion. They recognize the growing failures of the people and systems that govern our everyday lives.

Yet the underlying causes, effects, and corrective options often remain strangely difficult to clearly identify, explain, or even discuss. Not because ordinary people are incapable of understanding them, but because modern politics constantly overwhelms, distracts, distorts, and blurs the picture.

This work is my attempt to bring the picture closer.

To simplify it.

To sharpen it.

And to help clarify what I believe is already sitting directly in front of us — that CommonSense Americans possess far more power than they have been conditioned to believe — the power to reclaim their self-government and restore it to its proper purpose: maximizing their freedom to pursue fulfilling, happy lives.

Introduction

Most Americans know something is wrong. They just don't know how to understand it, explain it, or fix it.

But they feel it in their daily lives — frustration with politics-as-usual, exhaustion from the constant conflict it provokes, and a quiet but clear sense that the system of governance meant to serve them has instead been working against them. They are told this is normal. That this is the best we can do — the most we can hope for — the way things just *are*.

And all that remains for them is this persistently simple but deeply unsatisfying choice: Bad… or worse?

This work rejects that premise while advancing four objectives:

First and foremost, to remind us of our self-government's true purpose — preserving and expanding our freedom to pursue fulfilling, happy lives. Government was never intended to be an end unto itself, but a means of ensuring that most basic purpose.

Second, to identify the forces that have distracted us from that purpose with a broken political system built on false choices and conditioned pessimism.

Third, to expose the failures, contradictions, and dangers of those forces — not through ideology, but through CommonSense principles and self-evident truth.

And Fourth, to show the way back to that purpose by demonstrating that better alternatives are not only possible, but practical — alternatives that reflect what most Americans already instinctively know to be fair, workable, and right.

It is to remind us that what we want today is the same thing we have always wanted — and that the notion that achieving it is somehow 'unrealistic' has been repeatedly disproven by our own history. In other words, we've done it before — we can do it again.

This is not a manifesto in search of allegiance.
It is not a protest to vent frustration.
It is not a theory that requires belief in something unproven.

It is a system upgrade — a CommonSense framework for understanding what has gone wrong, why it persists, and how it can be corrected.

Not someday, but now.

The ideas presented here are not new, and they are certainly not revolutionary. They are, in many ways, the oldest and most enduring of American ideals — updated for a modern world, stripped of unnecessary complexity, and returned to their practical purpose.

PART I: SELF-EVIDENT TRUTHS

"We hold these truths to be self-evident, that all men are created equal, that they are endowed by their Creator with certain unalienable Rights, that among these are Life, Liberty and the pursuit of Happiness.--That to secure these rights, Governments are instituted among Men, deriving their just powers from the consent of the governed, --That whenever any Form of Government becomes destructive of these ends, it is the Right of the People to alter or to abolish it, and to institute new Government, laying its foundation on such principles and organizing its powers in such form, as to them shall seem most likely to effect their Safety and Happiness. Prudence, indeed, will dictate that Governments long established should not be changed for light and transient causes; and accordingly all experience hath shewn, that mankind are more disposed to suffer, while evils are sufferable, than to right themselves by abolishing the forms to which they are accustomed. But when a long train of abuses and usurpations, pursuing invariably the same Object evinces a design to reduce them under absolute Despotism, it is their right, it is their duty, to throw off such Government, and to provide new Guards for their future security."

Those famous words from the Declaration of Independence are not true because Thomas Jefferson wrote them. Jefferson wrote them because they are true — *self-evidently true.*

There is no debating that our self-government is "instituted among" us to "secure" *life, liberty, and the pursuit of happiness.*

Genius that it was and still is, however, Jefferson's expression of that simple idea may have actually missed the mark just ever so slightly. For, while life and liberty are certainly "unalienable rights" in a sense, they are also means to the fundamental pursuit that follows. So too, in fact, is the "safety" government is meant to "effect" alongside that pursuit.

Human beings don't live just to live, and liberty and safety mean nothing without higher purpose.

Yes, these rights are foundational to American self-governance, but *only* because they assure us of the ability to engage in the daily pursuit of the singular idea that has united every single human being who has ever walked the face of the earth — *fulfilling, happy lives, free to the greatest extent possible from unjust interference.*

1. The CommonSense Majority

Most Americans are not ideologues. They are not activists, pundits, or political insiders. They are citizens with everyday lives to lead — families to support, careers to build, bills to pay.

Politics, for them, is not a point of civic pride — nor is it cause to hate their neighbors or feud with their families.

These days especially, it is a burdensome exercise in futility.

They pay attention when they must — voting not hopefully but defensively out of fear and a fading sense of civic duty.

They care about the direction of their country, the strength of their communities, and the opportunities available to them and their families — but they do not spend their days arguing over abstract theories or partisan narratives.

They are focused on daily life, further defined by instinct — an instinct for stability, for decency, for practicality, and for fairness.

They favor practical solutions — ideas that function in the real world, as opposed to grand promises of overnight success or theories from dusty textbooks. But they are not absolutists who insist on all or nothing

They are the vast *CommonSense Majority.*

And yet, despite numbering eight out of ten or more of us, they rarely feel represented.

Instead, they are consistently presented with false choices — choices that force them to support 'leaders' undeserving of their trust and policies that never quite match their true preferences.

They are told that practical compromise is weakness, that obvious answers are unrealistic, and that the only responsible choice is to pick the least bad side and defend it.

So they shrug… and comply.

Not out of conviction, not out of confidence, not out of optimism and hopefulness — but out of exhaustion.

They choose the *lesser of two evils.*

They participate in a system they do not trust or respect because they see no viable alternative. And over time, this pattern produces something more corrosive than disagreement: *quiet resignation.*

But this resignation should not be mistaken for indifference.

The CommonSense Majority is not silent because it has nothing to say. It is quiet because experience has taught it that speaking up rarely changes anything.

That must change.

2. We Agree

The CommonSense Majority's desires and beliefs are neither complicated nor difficult to understand. More importantly, they are widely shared.

Across polls, elections, and in everyday life, Americans consistently express a remarkably stable set of expectations about how their government should function and what it should deliver. These expectations are generally not aimed at one party or the other. In fact, they frequently cross party lines. Nor are they driven by ideology. They are practical standards — formed not in theory, but by lived experience.

Most Americans do not want conflict. They do not wake up looking for a fight. They are not interested in winning political arguments for their own sake. All they want is the freedom to live happy, everyday lives.

They want to trust that the rules they follow are applied evenly to everyone.

They want to believe that hard work and fair play will be rewarded.

They want to feel that their voice matters — that they are heard — that they can make a difference.

And when it comes to government, they want a system that makes these things more possible — not more difficult.

They want government to be effective, but limited. They expect it to perform its core responsibilities competently and reliably, but they do not want it intruding in every aspect of their lives.

They want clear, reasonable, and fairly enforced laws that treat everyone equally.

They want progress, but not so much so fast that stability in daily life suffers. Change is necessary and, in fact, inevitable — but excessive disruption can also be unsettling and counterproductive. Most Americans are not resistant to change. They are resistant to extreme upheaval that ignores consequences — consequences typically suffered mostly by them.

They want accountability, especially for those entrusted with power. When leaders abuse that trust there should be real, visible consequences. Without it — as we have seen — self-service too often displaces public duty.

And they want more civil persuasion and less coercion in the conduct of our politics. They do not want to be forced into agreement through pressure, fear, or manipulation. They want arguments that make sense, practical solutions that actually work, and respectful leadership that trusts *their* ability to think and decide for themselves.

These are not radical expectations. They are not even controversial. And because we agree on them so intuitively, they form the very foundation of our unity and strength — the foundation upon which we may rebuild and rededicate our purpose driven self-government.

PART II: THE OBSTACLES TO COMMONSENSE SELF-GOVERNANCE

1. The Corrupt Power Establishment

To understand why CommonSense governance remains seemingly out of reach, it is necessary to examine its root causes.

The most pervasive of these is what we call the *Corrupt Power Establishment.*

Not a shadowy cabal straight out of Hollywood.
Not a clandestine organization with secret membership.
Not a dark conspiracy functionally coordinated to rule the world.

Rather, it is a naturally occurring alignment of interests and influence among those who hold disproportionate power in American life — across politics, media, industry, religion, and academia.

These individuals and the institutions they lead do not wake up each day intending to subjugate the public. Like all people, they operate largely within accepted legal and ethical boundaries. Mostly, they mean well.

They pursue success, stability, advancement, and happiness — just like the rest of us.

But collectively, their incentives combined with outsized resources and influence point in a direction that consistently advantages them while systematically disadvantaging the rest.

They benefit from systems that preserve their status at the expense of the masses.

They benefit from complexity that limits public oversight.

They benefit from influence that is self-reinforcing and resistant to challenge.

And over time, these incentives produce predictably troublesome outcomes.

Policies grow more complex — and less transparent.
Decision-making becomes more distant — and less accountable.
Public debate becomes more performative — and less substantive.

And everyday life for most of us becomes more difficult — and less fulfilling.

Because this concentration of disproportionate power resides within a small fraction of the population, it is typically sustained indirectly — through forced attention, controlled narrative, and artificial division.

When public attention is directed toward constant controversy, deeper structural problems go unnoticed.

When issues are framed in ways that emphasize conflict over resolution, practical alternatives remain out of view — and out of reach.

And when citizens are divided into opposing camps, their collective power and leverage disappears.

For the CommonSense Majority, this creates a persistent disconnect.

They may participate in the system — but they do not feel represented by it.

They are significantly affected by decisions — but they have limited influence over them.

They are regularly assured that they are in control — but they sense only powerlessness.

This is the perversion of politics and self-government in America today.

It's less about illegal or even intentional misconduct and more about a structural misalignment of social, political, and cultural incentives — one that produces results that consistently favor the few over the many.

Until that misalignment is recognized for what it is — the predictable product of a naturally occurring Corrupt Power Establishment — it cannot be corrected.

2. UnCompromising Extremism

If the Corrupt Power Establishment explains how influence is naturally concentrated and systematically abused, *UnCompromising Extremism* explains how that concentration and abuse are enabled in plain sight.

UnCompromising Extremism is not defined by ideology. It exists on all sides of the political spectrum and is defined by method.

It insists that every issue has only two acceptable positions — diametrically opposed, mutually exclusive, and morally absolute.

It rejects practical compromise, not as a strategic choice, but as a principle.

And it treats disagreement not as civil debate to be thoughtfully resolved, but as existential threat to be defeated at all cost.

In this framework, there are no trade-offs.
No legitimate opposing views.
No hope for cooperation, reconciliation, and unity.

Only total victory or complete surrender.

As a governing approach, this produces predictable results.

Problems remain unresolved because workable solutions are dismissed as insufficient.

Policies swing dramatically when power shifts, only to be reversed again later.

And precious energy is wasted on meaningless arguments instead of advancing worthwhile progress.

Over time, this creates a cycle of destructive escalation — each side hardening its position, each victory temporary, each defeat fueling the next confrontation.

But the impact of UnCompromising Extremism extends well beyond these surface level effects. It plays a critical role in sustaining the broader political ecosystem described earlier.

When public debate is dominated by extremes, the range of acceptable solutions narrows. Citizens are forced to choose between positions that do not reflect their views. The CommonSense Majority disappears from the conversation — not because it lacks ideas or inherent power, but because those ideas are excluded from the debate and that power suppressed beyond recognition.

In this way, UnCompromising Extremism becomes a highly effective tool for the Corrupt Power Establishment.

Not necessarily by design.
Not always by intent.
But consistently in effect.

It reinforces the conditions under which concentrated power remains insulated:

By keeping everyday citizens distracted and divided, limiting their collective influence.

By keeping attention focused on controversy and conflict, rather than structural integrity.

It ensures that alternatives outside the binary extremes are rarely considered, and even more rarely implemented.

While extremists on opposing sides see themselves as adversaries, they actually share a fundamental alignment.

They both rely on conflict to maintain relevance.

They both depend on the absence of middle-ground solutions.

And they both seek a system where power, once gained, can be exercised with minimal restraint.

This is why their behavior often appears hypocritical.

Positions once condemned are later adopted.
Those once defended are later ignored.

The objective is not principled purpose — it is control.

For the CommonSense Majority, the effect is disorienting.

They are told these are the only choices.
They are told compromise is unacceptable.
They are told that rejecting both sides inevitably serves the greater evil.

So again, they comply — not because they agree, but because they see no alternative.

UnCompromising Extremism does not just distort outcomes. It distorts the field of possibility itself.

Until that distortion is recognized — and rejected — the majority will continue to be force-fed unsatisfactory options.

3. Radical Realism

If the system produces outcomes most Americans do not want, and if those outcomes persist over time, another question is raised:

Why do people continue to accept it?

The answer lies in a mindset that has quietly overpowered CommonSense Americans — a mindset we call *Radical Realism.*

Radical Realism is the belief that the dysfunction of modern politics is not only unavoidable, but literally unchangeable. It sounds practical, and it passes for learned experience. And in that sense, it masquerades as wisdom beyond dispute.

But at its core, it is something else — something dark and unworthy of a great people:

It is defeatism, rationalized.

Most Americans will readily acknowledge that the system is flawed. They see the division, the inconsistency, the lack of accountability. They recognize that outcomes rarely reflect what is necessary, effective, and fair.

And yet, when presented with the possibility of meaningful change, familiar objections are all too often reflexively raised:

"That's not realistic."
"That's not how it works."
"That will never happen."

These reactions are not rooted in objective analysis of what is actually possible. They are rooted in repeated exposure to what has been — and the irrational belief that what has been will always be.

Over time, patterns become expectations.
Expectations become assumptions.
And assumptions become limits.

Radical Realism takes those patterns, expectations, and limits and presents them as permanent.

It does not argue that the system is working well.
It argues that it simply cannot work any other way.

This is what makes it so powerful.

It requires no coordination from smoke-filled back rooms. It naturally affirms itself.

And it serves the interests of both forces described earlier.

For the Corrupt Power Establishment, Radical Realism protects the status quo that serves it so well. If people believe meaningful change is unrealistic, they are far less likely to demand it in the first place. Consequently, important structural questions go unasked, and deeper reforms go unexplored.

For UnCompromising Extremists, it preserves the binary. If no practical alternative is considered viable, then the only options left are the polar opposites they define. The conflict continues, and with it, their relevance.

Though these forces often appear to be in strict opposition, Radical Realism quietly serves them both.

It limits creative problem solving.
It discourages pragmatic initiative.
It narrows the very field of possibility.

And for the CommonSense Majority, its effects are profound.

Civic engagement becomes depressed.

Steadily declining participation is reduced to convictionless habit.

Hopes and expectations for the future dissolve in the face of past experience.

So they tell themselves that politics is separate from their daily lives — willfully blinding themselves to the opposite truth, even as its effects shape those daily lives in clearly tangible ways.

What began as skepticism has become acceptance.
What started as frustration has become resignation.

Radical Realism is not realism at all.

It is a conditioned, self-limitation — a way of thinking that confuses what is common with what is possible — to the complete and utter neglect of what is preferred and, in fact, necessary.

It argues against hope. But more than that, it does so in a way that makes hope feel foolish.

Until that belief is rejected, no structural reform, no political realignment, and no CommonSense alternative can fully advance.

Because before the system can change, the false assumptions that currently sustain it must be discarded.

4. The False Choice Paradigm

In modern American politics, one powerful assumption — rarely stated, but constantly reinforced — lies at the heart of its widely perceived dysfunction:

That for every important issue, there are only two realistic options.

Two positions.
Two paths.
Two sides to choose from.

This assumption shapes everything that follows. It defines how issues are framed, how debates are conducted, and how decisions are ultimately made. It turns complex questions into binary contests and reduces governance to a series of increasingly unsatisfying, forced choices.

But it isn't true.

The reality is simpler — and far more consequential:

Most of the choices presented to the American people are incomplete.

They are not the full range of available options. They are carefully crafted — limited, amplified, and then repeated until they appear exhaustive.

And because they are presented as the *only* options, they are inevitably treated as such.

This is the *False Choice Paradigm* — the preferred tool of UnCompromising Extremists alluded to previously.

The False Choice Paradigm does not require deception in the traditional sense. It operates through expectation, reinforcement, and repetition — the very conditions that give rise to its close relative, Radical Realism.

Together, these forces form a self-affirming cycle: the narrowing of choices produces the belief that no alternatives exist — and that belief, in turn, sustains and justifies the ongoing narrowing of choices.

Whether designed or not, those who benefit from this cycle consistently recognize its utility and act in ways that fortify it. And the result over time is clear and critical: people stop looking for alternatives — not because they don't actually exist, but because they are conditioned to *believe* they do not.

CommonSense Americans recognize all of this instinctively.

They understand that the options presented rarely reflect the path they seek. They can see, often immediately, that a more practical approach *should* be available — one that stays true to their guiding interests rather than getting sidetracked with petty partisan power struggles.

But because that option is not formally offered, it is dismissed outright.

Not debated.
Not refined.
Not tested.

Simply excluded.

Rejecting the False Choice Paradigm requires a fundamental change of mindset. Not only must we refuse to accept that the usual binary options are the only ones that exist — even as they continue to be the only ones offered. But we must also recognize that the CommonSense solutions we would prefer are something more than the midpoints between those opposite views.

They are independent of the extremes and stand entirely on their own — built from first principles, informed by reality, and judged by practical outcomes rather than ideology and partisan gain.

That is where the real opportunity emerges.

When citizens begin to question the boundaries of the debate itself, the sturdy structure of the warped system begins to loosen. New ideas emerge — not as theoretical constructs, but as practical responses to problems that were never adequately addressed.

The effect is immediate.

What once appeared natural begins to look artificial.
What once seemed inevitable begins to look optional.
And what once felt impossible begins to feel achievable.

This is the first step toward restoring control to the majority and America to the path most of us want but have long given up on — not by choosing more carefully between the options given, but by ensuring better options altogether.

Because the moment the False Choice Paradigm is rejected, real hope for the happy lives we instinctively desire immediately rekindles.

PART III: THE KEYS TO MEANINGFUL CHANGE

1. Recommitting to Principle and Purpose

Recognizing and rejecting the obstacles to CommonSense governance revives hope and reopens the path most Americans want but have long been denied. But hope and opportunity are just a start. From there, the real work of rebuilding our self-governance begins — with the re-establishment of a firm foundation of principle.

Because today's politics has become inverted.

Like a pyramid balanced precariously on its point, instead of policy being built on a solid base of enduring principles, those policies are now routinely redefined as principles themselves — to justify political positions and arguments.

But positions shift with power. Arguments shift with advantage. What is defended one day is denounced the next.

And our upside down system tips.

Because the shifting political positions and the policies they spawn are not, in fact, principles.

They are partisan gamesmanship.

And when the pursuit of party advantage takes precedence over commitment to principle, the very purpose of our nation gets lost — because our principles and purpose are actually one and the same.

We believe in the principle of free expression — so we constantly strive to defend it.

We believe in the principle of equality — so we constantly struggle to promote it.

We believe in the principle of individual liberty — so we constantly press to expand it.

All adding up to our ultimate purpose — the free pursuit of happy lives.

Principle and purpose.

Recommitting to principle and purpose requires the enforcement of consistent standards, regardless of circumstance or partisan favor — not only when it's convenient, but especially when it is not.

This is where credibility and trust are established and true progress enabled.

It's easy to defend free expression when it protects views you agree with.

It's far more difficult when it protects views you oppose.

It's easy to promote equality when you stand to gain.

It's far more difficult when it means forfeiting established advantage.

And it's easy to press for expanding individual liberty when the other side is in control.

But far more difficult when it requires you to cede accumulated government power.

These are the tests that matter most.

Principles that apply only when they are convenient are not principles at all. They are excuses — ends that do little more than justify means.

Therefore, at every turn we must ask ourselves – do the policies under debate reflect our true principles and, in that way, promise the practical advancement of our fundamental purpose?

Or do they merely represent yet another costly detour that will ultimately amount to wasted time, energy, and resources?

Recommitting to principle and purpose does not eliminate disagreement over details. It does, however, clarify those details, ensuring that the debate moves in the direction we all wish to go.

It allows citizens to evaluate arguments based on substance rather than source.

It forces leaders to act with consistency rather than calculation.

And it creates the conditions under which CommonSense persuasion — rather than partisan pressure — can be restored as the primary force in our politics.

These principles establish how decisions can and should be measured — not by who benefits in the moment, but by whether the outcome aligns with that foundational purpose.

Because without our recommitment to this purpose and the principles that support it, America's system of self-governance will continue to tip.

But with it, meaningful progress becomes possible once again.

2. Reprioritizing Persuasion Over Force

If principle defines what we stand for, *persuasion* determines the sustainability of our efforts.

You can force people to go along with something, or you can persuade them.

In politics and governance, force can work — for a while. It can push policies through, win short-term victories, and create the *appearance* of progress.

But it doesn't last.

Eventually, people push back — sometimes even when the underlying policy has merit. Resistance to imposed authority is that deeply embedded in the American character.

We've seen that cycle play out again and again.

One side wins.
It assumes an exaggerated mandate and rushes to assert authority.
It goes too far too fast, and the voters push back by shifting power to the other.
The other side makes the same mistake — and the cycle repeats.

Real progress — the kind that lasts — only happens when people willingly buy in. When they understand something, agree with it, and accept it as fair, even if it's not ideal.

That kind of agreement doesn't come from the pressure of the False Choice Paradigm. It comes from trust.

And trust comes from a few basic concepts:

Telling the truth, even when it's inconvenient.
Listening, even when you disagree.
Being open to practical compromise, even when it may *feel* like abandoning principles.

That's how a healthy system is supposed to work.

Leaders make their case.
Citizens weigh it.
And decisions are made with broad enough support to hold over time.

Right now, we're not doing that.

Leaders keep offering their false choices, characterizing their adversary as the greater evil.

We succumb to the "reality" of those false choices and meekly fall in line.

And decisions are made that genuinely satisfy a mere fraction of us, assuring their reversal upon the next wishful campaign promise.

For those leaders, perpetuating this volatile cycle — even though it means constantly trading power and control — is preferable to the hard work of earning broad support.

Because it's faster, and it's easier — and politicians instinctively favor the path of least resistance.

But it's also weaker.

Because anything built that way can be torn down just as quickly.

Persuasion takes longer. It requires patience. It requires effort. And it requires leaders to respect and trust the people — a critical component that has been missing for too long.

But it's absolutely essential in a free country.

You can't have self-government without consent. And you can't have true consent without honest persuasion.

That's the standard.

Not who can push harder.
Not who can shout louder.
Not who can scare more effectively.

But who can make the better case — and make it in a way that people are willing to accept, stand behind, and see through.

When that happens, everything changes.

Tensions ease.
Consensus builds.
Decisions hold.

And finally, our self-doubt evaporates and our eyes open to the reality of our power — to demand and achieve the change we truly want.

3. Removing Self-Doubt

Despite broad and persistent consensus about what CommonSense Americans want and expect from their government, those ideas rarely influence political action or public debate.

Instead, they are overshadowed — pushed aside by extreme voices that demand something else, while portraying divisive conflict as inevitable and practical compromise as surrender.

So we allow a loud few to overwhelm the strength of that consensus and, in so doing, we undermine ourselves.

In other words, most of us agree on most matters, but we allow extremists to convince us we don't.

Recognizing that is the first step toward resolving it.

When we take that step, we will begin to see the reality of our power — and the power of our reality.

We will be jolted awake by the recollection of America's purpose — its intended design to serve *our* shared, CommonSense interests.

We will awaken — and we will act.

Until that time, however, the quiet frustration beneath our acceptance will remain.

On issue after issue, we will continue to be forced into false choices between opposing extremes — framed as right versus wrong, all or nothing, total victory or total defeat.

Accept one. Reject the other. Choose a side.

We will continue to ignore the CommonSense wisdom of the whispering voice that tells us it's all wrong — that a more balanced, practical alternative not only *should* be available but, in fact, *is* available — if only we could muster the strength and the will to open our eyes to it.

These frustrations will remain — and they will grow.

And even as we begin to recognize that better options may exist, we further undermine ourselves with the pernicious belief that they simply are not realistic under current conditions.

It's a belief that comes not from indifference, but from repetition.

Those same false choices forced upon us again and again — elections framed as polar opposites, debates that leave little room for nuance, results that satisfy few but are celebrated by those few as decisive victories.

Over time, our acceptance deepens — and our expectations recede.

We accept trade-offs we would otherwise question.
We tolerate outcomes we do not fully believe in.
We participate less, and with less conviction — and, gradually, with less hope.

This is the ongoing erosion of America's political condition.

The CommonSense Majority knows what it wants but undermines itself by doubting its own strength — and the system's ability to deliver.

That doubt is what holds us back — overcoming it is what will set us free.

PART IV: COMMONSENSE SELF-GOVERNANCE IN PRACTICE

1. Power's Rightful Place

In a country as large and diverse as the United States, it's no surprise that a one-size-fits-all approach to public policy seldom works well.

What is effective in one region may be unnecessary or counterproductive in another. What makes sense in one state may not make sense in another. What works in densely populated urban centers may not work in more sparsely populated rural communities.

And yet, over time, we have allowed policymaking power to steadily migrate upward — away from the places where we actually live and into a distant national bureaucracy.

The results are evident all around us:

Policymakers who are out of touch with and unresponsive to local needs.

Rules that are overly rigid and resistant to constructive change.

Programs that promise increased security and freedom but deliver neither.

And citizens who feel increasingly disconnected from the policy decisions that shape their daily lives.

CommonSense demands the reversal of that trend.

That doesn't mean everything belongs at the local level — but it does mean decision-making power should default there unless a clear and compelling national interest requires otherwise.

To be sure, the objective is not blind decentralization. It is practical alignment — locating problem-solvers and the resources they require closer to the people they exist to serve and the problems they're designed to resolve.

Because when public policy is made closer to home — closer to the people directly affected — it just works better.

Problems can be more easily identified and their impact on daily life better understood.

Citizens can more easily engage the process and the decision-makers.

Ideas can be more quickly tested and their effectiveness more clearly observed.

Adjustments can be more efficiently implemented and more accurately evaluated.

And public resources can be more responsibly managed and the spenders held more accountable.

That clarity matters.

The most common source of frustration in American life is not disagreement over policy itself, but confusion about accountability. When something goes wrong, the logical questions are always:

"Who did this?"
"How did it happen?"
"What can be done to fix it?"

In our top-down, sprawling bureaucratic system, those questions are too often difficult to answer.

Responsibilities have become blurred between federal agencies, courts, presidents, Congress, state governments, local officials, and overlapping bureaucracies that cast blame endlessly between one another. Authority and responsibility are constantly pushed and pulled between levels of government according to shifting political incentives.

Federal officials routinely pull power upward when doing so expands politically desirable control, while pushing responsibility downward when the political cost of that control is too high. State and local officials often engage in the opposite behavior — pushing politically difficult problems upward while pulling authority downward whenever greater local control becomes profitable.

In the end, meaningful accountability to the people disappears in the fog.

That is when citizens begin losing confidence not only in their leaders and policies, but in self-government itself.

A CommonSense system restores clarity by assigning authority to where it best belongs.

At the federal level, power should be limited primarily to matters that are truly national in scope:

Protecting the nation from external threats.

Safeguarding constitutional rights and liberties equally for all Americans.

Coordinating interstate activity where national uniformity is genuinely necessary.

And representing the United States and its interests abroad with one unified voice.

Conversely, most domestic policy should reside at the state level. States are large enough to manage complexity, but still small enough to represent the differing values, priorities, and practical realities of their populations. They can adapt, experiment, compete, and learn from one another more swiftly and in ways centralized systems rarely can.

At the local level, government should focus on the issues people experience most directly in everyday life — education, policing, infrastructure maintenance, healthcare, and environmental protection — where proximity produces both responsiveness and more immediate accountability.

Government today reflects too little of this organization. Again, it is far too common practice for the federal government to dictate local policies by broadly asserting national interests — and it is just as common for local authorities to slough their responsibilities upward to excuse their own failures and evade accountability.

But when government is more properly and carefully organized from the bottom up, communities naturally begin to improve through trial and error, competition, and shared best practices.

Across 50 states and countless cities and towns, citizens — all striving toward the same basic goal of happier, more fulfilling lives — will employ all their experience, wisdom, and talent in pursuit of the most effective public policies for that purpose. Successful ideas will spread rapidly. Failed approaches will be efficiently exposed and discarded just as rapidly.

In the end, states and local communities — freed from the bureaucratic paralysis inherent in sprawling centralized systems — will adopt what works and move away from what doesn't as a natural reaction to actual lived experience.

Such practical competition in a vibrant free marketplace of ideas is healthy. It keeps systems honest. It prevents stagnation. And it creates constant positive pressure to improve without the wasteful baggage of distant, detached micromanagement.

Perhaps most importantly, this structure offers the greatest opportunity for widespread success and satisfaction because it recognizes a CommonSense reality:

Communities should not have to suffer prolonged negative consequences when one-size-fits-all policies serve others at their expense.

Successful public policy need not function as a zero-sum game. One "winning" community does not necessitate one that loses. With greater local control — perhaps even with occasional, carefully restrained *assists* from Washington — all communities can prosper.

A strong nation — comprised of healthy, vibrant, happy local communities — does not require uniformity in every decision.

It requires a flexible structure where better ideas rise naturally, failed ones are discarded quickly, and citizens retain meaningful influence over the policies that shape their everyday lives.

Government redesigned this way — where citizens control and exercise greater authority closer to home — is the best way to maximize benefit, limit dysfunction, and restore confidence in self-government itself.

It is where power belongs.

2. Checks and Balances

Independent of any shift of authority from Washington to the states, we must endeavor to restore proper balance to that which remains between the federal government's constitutional power centers.

That system was brilliantly designed with a self-enforcing failsafe against the abuse of power — the establishment of three coequal branches to direct its functions, each fundamentally enabled to oversee and check the power of the others. Congress would make the laws. The president would implement them. And the courts would interpret and enforce them. Each would be endowed with institutional responsibility and incentive to ensure that the others did not exceed their respective mandates.

That structure still exists on paper. But in practice, it has fallen dangerously out of balance.

Over time, too much legislative power has drifted into the executive branch — into faceless rule-making agencies, departments, and administrative systems that most people seldom ever see and never directly vote for.

In other words, into the hands of an unelected, unaccountable bureaucracy.

Instead of clearly written and openly debated laws and policies, many of the rules that shape daily life now come from these overly complex regulatory systems — which too often produce negative consequences that seem much harder to undo than they are to enact in the first place.

This is one more source of Americans' growing dissatisfaction.

Presidents may be faulted for their over-accumulation of power and mismanagement of it — but the failure especially lies at the feet of the other two branches for allowing it to happen. Even more, it rests with a system that has somehow morphed into a do-it-all monstrosity where all sides constantly point fingers at the others and none take responsibility for fixing it.

So once again, it is left to us — *We the People.*

Reducing and refocusing the federal government's role to its core functions will go a long way toward minimizing the effects of continued operational failures — but not far enough. To return to a government optimized for supporting a truly free people, best efforts must be aimed at restoring congressional accountability, reining in the power of the imperial presidency, and reforming judicial authority.

Reasserting Congressional Accountability

By definition, law amounts to nothing more than a trade of individual liberty for the promise of order and security — fundamental necessities to our ongoing pursuit of happy lives. It's a delicate balance, however, as each new law reduces our freedom just a little more, even as the benefits we're paying for often become less clear.

Historically, government has been very effective at this business — selling us the *promise* of order and security, that is.

It is in its very nature.

But in the second half of the eighteenth century, America's founders came to recognize an even greater hidden cost beyond the price of everyday liberty most people willingly paid: it's corrosive impact on the very pursuit it was supposed to enhance.

This realization struck them so profoundly that they decided to risk everything — their "lives, fortunes, and sacred honor" — in support of it through a long-shot revolt and a revolutionary new system of self-government. And when their enormous sacrifice yielded victory, they moved decisively to build a constitutional order with that singular purpose permanently cemented into its foundation.

And at the center of its design? The Congress — where the *"People's House"* of Representatives would forever protect and ensure our experiment in self-government.

Contrary to modern misconceptions, however, Congress was never intended to function as an efficient machine for mass-producing legislation. In fact, it was intentionally structured to do almost the opposite.

The founders deeply distrusted concentrated government power because history had repeatedly demonstrated its tendency toward abuse. So, they devised a legislative body *deliberately restrained* by competing interests, layered representation, procedural friction, and slow-moving consensus-building.

Lawmaking was intentionally made difficult because every new law represented an expansion of government authority and a corresponding reduction in individual liberty — the very thing our ancestors valued most.

Congress, therefore, was designed less as an engine of constant action than as a guardian against *unnecessary* government action.

Its constitutional role was to protect that freedom to pursue happiness by exercising power cautiously, deliberately, and *only* when broad public consensus deemed it absolutely necessary.

That restraint was not a bug in the system — it was a primary feature.

But over time, America's political culture began to change — and so did Congress's approach.

Evolving mass media, instant communication, and increasingly nationalized politics gave rise to growing public demand for immediate federal responses to nearly every problem or controversy — a misguided call for government intervention into virtually every aspect of daily life.

Constitutional restraint came to be viewed not as prudence, but as paralysis.

Deliberation became dysfunction.

Institutional friction became incompetent failure.

And the question suddenly morphed from the skeptical:
"Is this really a problem for government to solve?"

to one that assumed it as a given based upon a simple linguistic misinterpretation:
"Why aren't lawmakers doing their jobs and making more laws?"

Caught between a constitutional structure intentionally designed to slow the exercise of too-easily-corruptible power and a political culture demanding immediate results, Congress quickly adapted to its changing incentives.

Rather than defending restraint and limited government, too many politicians chose instead to follow the prevailing political winds and embraced the untenable notion that a strong central government can and should solve virtually every problem.

And when that proved to be more difficult than expected, members of Congress quickly discovered that they profited more from public displays of partisan combat than the difficult work of upholding their constitutional duty.

The representatives of the people forgot the people they were supposed to be representing.

This led to frustrated political factions also buying in to a top down, do-it-all central government — increasingly turning to presidents and the courts to achieve through unilateral action what Congress either could not or would not enact legislatively.

Oblivious to the long-term ramifications of its retreat, Congress breathed a sigh of relief.

Because allowing presidents and judges to assume greater responsibility and visibility enabled legislators to avoid accountability themselves. Rhetorically gifted politicians could take undue credit for popular outcomes, while condemning the failure of presidents, courts, and partisan adversaries for unpopular ones. Suddenly — mercifully — difficult governing became someone else's problem.

It was a profound unbalancing of carefully constructed constitutional power.

By acquiescing to the expansion of executive authority, Congress weakened itself and unwittingly opened government to the vulnerability of the legislative overreach it was designed to prevent.

Clothed in the promise of *easier* accountability, what actually resulted was an executive leadership model that would prove more responsive to ideological extremes than practical, everyday citizens — leading to political and cultural instability, perpetually heightened civic conflict and, ironically, *less* accountability to the CommonSense Majority.

Today, those political consequences are in plain view.

Executive Orders routinely substitute for legislation — and change dramatically and abruptly from one administration to the next.

National politics revolve almost entirely around presidential conflict — and the fight to claim and wield that power.

Every election is framed as existential — lest the opposition prevail and redirect or cement their policies in the opposite extreme.

And all the while, Congress continues to disown its constitutional responsibilities — choosing instead to act more as detached pundits than guardians of the people's liberty.

But this dysfunction did not emerge by accident.

Today's politics and government were intentionally altered to strengthen the control of the nation's two major political parties and the broader political establishment around them. And in the process, candidates and incumbents alike were overwhelmingly incentivized to adopt rigid party dogma and engage in uncompromising political warfare in order to advance their careers.

Americans understand that members of Congress are supposed to represent the will of the majority in their districts — and that their need for our votes in general elections is what should ensure their responsiveness to our expectations and demands.

They also understand, however, that this is seldom how the system actually works.

In reality, most members answer almost exclusively to the small faction of hyper-partisan activists most immediately consequential to their political survival — the UnCompromising Extremists who comprise the bases of the two parties.

It's a dynamic that exists because more than nine out of ten congressional districts today have been carefully engineered to be politically *safe*. In other words, general elections — where the CommonSense Majority correctly perceives its natural opportunity to directly enforce democratic accountability — no longer act as incentive for politicians to represent the true will of the people, because the outcome of most of those elections is effectively decided before the first ballot is cast.

Instead, today's real battlegrounds for political power and control — where professional politicians strive to ensure lengthy political careers — are the low turnout, high intensity party primary elections which are dominated by those partisan zealots.

Satisfying extremists rather than representing the practical interests of the broader public has become our political system's modern day fault line. It divides us and increasingly shakes the ground beneath our feet.

And it's the perverse incentive that holds the key to understanding today's most fundamental problems with America's government. Therefore, it must be the main focus of our attention and efforts to reclaim control over government and its impact on our daily lives.

But because this system protects incumbents in *both* parties, we cannot count on the people operating within it to help reform it voluntarily.

Just as our ancestors did in 1776, we must take control and fix it ourselves.

Fortunately, this complex problem points directly to its own practical solution. If perverted political incentives created our broken system, properly realigned incentives can correct it.

Those proper incentives can and must be addressed through CommonSense election reform.

Proposals like party-neutral congressional redistricting, party-neutral primaries, and party-neutral balloting are not procedural technicalities. They are mechanisms for taking power and control away from extremist dominated political parties and restoring it to the broader public.

They would virtually guarantee more competitive elections which would, in turn, force representatives to appeal once again to the CommonSense Majority.

That shift would not magically perfect Congress. But it would quickly and materially change politicians' governing behavior.

Because one thing will always be curiously true: the business of politics is actually one that is ultra-responsive to the free marketplace demands of engaged consumers.

And in a new world where political parties' hold on elections is loosened, the vast majority of those engaged consumers will once again be CommonSense voters.

In that world, challenger candidates will gain greater opportunity to educate and mobilize voters.

Incumbents will find it harder to evade responsibility.

And Congress will once again face meaningful pressure to produce practical results rather than mere displays of party loyalty.

Because when electoral systems reward extremism, extremism grows. But when those same systems reward practical governance, consensus-building, and CommonSense responsibility, political behavior will quickly redirect that way instead.

The path forward, therefore, involves neither blind faith in politicians nor cynical surrender to dysfunction.

It requires structural reform driven by engaged citizens who understand both the purpose of self-government and the proper incentives required to sustain it.

Congress holds enormous constitutional responsibilities, including taxing, appropriating public funds, and authorizing war. Those powers were never intended to be casually surrendered to presidents, bureaucracies, or ideological factions.

They were intended to remain strictly accountable to the people.

Restoring that accountability will not eliminate all disagreement — but it will lead to a legislative branch once again dedicated to the vigilant defense of individual liberty so essential to our free pursuit of happy lives.

Reining in the Imperial Presidency

When Congress succumbed to popular pressure for expansive government, it quickly realized that its structural design prevented it from exercising the power that expansion required.

But instead of understanding, accepting, and upholding that as the brilliant wisdom behind the founders' intent, it responded in the worst possible way — by forsaking its constitutional duty to keep overall government power in check and bestowing virtually unlimited authority to America's chief executive.

Like Caesar, presidents have been only too willing to accept it.

Faced with that same public demand for forceful action — and with little regard to future implications — presidents of both parties moved rapidly to expand that authority even further. They discarded Washington's example of self-restraint and began to aggressively exploit broadly enabling legalese — like *"emergency powers"* — as loopholes that afford them the ability to do virtually anything they want.

It was the advent of America's imperial presidency.

Not a dictatorship. Not even the product of malicious intent.

Simply the precise result the founders feared and worked so hard to prevent — the unleashing of dangerous, unchecked government power.

Once again, the effects are unmistakable:

Unelected bureaucrats writing and implementing vast numbers of rules with the force of law.

Executive Orders increasingly substituting for legislation.

Policies so imposed quickly and reversed just as quickly by successive administrations.

Public trust eroding as authority becomes increasingly centralized and volatile.

All together it amounts to tremendous instability throughout government — instability that has become disruptive and threatening in many ways to everyday life for all of us. And neither a hyper-partisan, overly deferential Congress nor a strict constructionist, hands-off Supreme Court has been inclined to step in.

Meanwhile, We the People hardly notice — and those that do largely approve.

It is not difficult to understand why.

The legislative process is cumbersome by design. Hundreds of elected officials — representing different states, regions, interests, and constituencies — negotiate endlessly over laws and policies that most citizens have neither the time nor patience to follow in detail. The process is slow. Complicated. Frustrating.

But mostly, it feels *unaccountable.*

By contrast, the thought of one national leader standing before us promising progress holds tremendous natural appeal.

One voice.
One agenda.
One person to credit — one person to blame.

Simple.

And at times, this concentration of responsibility has appeared to work well — thanks to exceptional leaders of great character, principle, and discipline who resisted the temptation to overreach.

More often, however, it has faltered — and we should not be surprised.

It's a recurring theme in any bureaucratic organization — especially the largest ones: the *law of unintended consequences.*

Americans have turned increasingly to authoritative presidents in the hopes that an individual so empowered could cut through government's size and complexity and make it work. And if he fails to do so, they simply replace him at the next election.

It's the natural hope for direct democratic accountability.

But what we have instead is something very different: today's completely broken politics where perpetual conflict and dissatisfaction is the norm — and our daily lives suffer.

By investing so much power and expectation in the presidency — expectations that are virtually impossible for any one person to meet — Americans inadvertently turned presidential politics into an existential battlefield where the fighting never lets up.

Because how could it?

How could the fighting ease when UnCompromising Extremists — fueled by a belief that the president's is the only power that matters and amplified by 24-hour tabloid media — tell us constantly that every presidential decision, act, and utterance carries the potential to either save or destroy our nation?

That's the trap in which the CommonSense Majority finds itself today. It has allowed the empowerment of an ineffectual chief executive while, at the same time, falling under the illusory spell that the battle of extremes over that one person is unavoidable.

And even when CommonSense Americans recognize that no president can truly succeed under these conditions, what are they left with?

Yet another false choice reinforced by UnCompromising Extremism and sustained by the Corrupt Power Establishment that benefits from perpetual conflict — bad or worse. Which one is least likely to destroy America?

CommonSense Americans are exhausted by the never-ending fight and continuing failure to address the issues that matter most to them. But by reining in the imperial presidency — and our unrealistic expectations of it — by clarifying and imposing strict, clear limits on its powers, we can begin to alleviate that fatigue and return our focus and energy to government's fundamental purpose.

Redefining Judicial Authority

America's courts were never intended to function as super-legislatures.

Their constitutional role was narrower, though no less important: to interpret the law, resolve disputes under it, and ensure that government itself remained bound by constitutional limits. The judiciary was designed to serve as a stabilizing force within the constitutional system — not as an independent political power center directing national policy according to the evolving preferences of judges.

But like the presidency, judicial authority has expanded far beyond its intended boundaries.

Today, courts increasingly intervene in disputes that are fundamentally political in nature — not merely interpreting law but effectively determining major public policy outcomes themselves. Judges are now routinely asked to settle controversies that the elected branches either refuse or are unable to resolve through the constitutional process. And in doing so, courts have gradually assumed powers never actually granted to them.

This has produced a dangerous distortion of democratic accountability.

Americans now regularly find themselves waiting for unelected judges to determine the meaning, application, or even practical existence of laws enacted by elected representatives.

Policies debated publicly and seemingly settled for years can suddenly be transformed, delayed, or invalidated through judicial interpretation alone.

Constitutional language long understood one way can abruptly be reinterpreted another — often throwing institutions and everyday people instantly into turmoil.

Whether one agrees with any specific ruling is almost beside the point.

When major policy decisions increasingly depend upon judicial interpretation rather than legislative clarity and democratic consensus, citizens naturally begin to feel disconnected from their own government. Accountability becomes blurred. Responsibility becomes difficult to locate. And public trust steadily erodes.

The courts did not create this dynamic alone.

Once again, the deeper failure originated in the political branches.

Congress increasingly passed vague, overly broad, and politically evasive legislation — often intentionally leaving difficult questions unresolved. Presidents increasingly relied on sweeping executive actions that pushed constitutional boundaries and invited legal challenge.

The result is a judiciary drawn ever deeper into partisan conflict and public suspicion — one that has become the final arbiter of disputes the constitutional system originally expected elected officials to resolve themselves.

Today, judicial nominations themselves often resemble political warfare because both parties increasingly view control of the courts as a substitute for durable legislative consensus. If laws cannot survive democratic disagreement, political factions instead seek judges willing to impose outcomes through interpretation.

That is not healthy for a free society.

Courts function best when they are viewed as legitimate referees carefully applying stable law — not as ideological warriors constantly fighting political battles. Restoring proper judicial balance therefore requires reform in several areas simultaneously.

First, laws themselves must become far clearer and more precise.

Vague legislation invites judicial expansion because ambiguity necessarily transfers interpretive power to courts and bureaucracies. Congress must reclaim its constitutional role and accept responsibility for writing laws that clearly define both meaning and limits rather than outsourcing difficult decisions to regulators and judges.

Second, the judicial appointments process must be reoriented toward institutional restraint rather than ideological combat.

At present, judicial confirmation battles increasingly revolve around projecting how nominees may rule on future political controversies. That dynamic further politicizes the courts while undermining public confidence in judicial neutrality. A healthier system would place greater emphasis on demonstrated constitutional discipline, judicial modesty, and consistent interpretive methodology rather than anticipated partisan policy outcomes.

Third, lifetime tenure should be reconsidered.

Lifetime judicial appointments were originally intended to protect judicial independence from temporary political pressure. But in modern practice, they have become a means for cementing partisan political advantage for decades. Regularized judicial turnover through fixed terms would preserve independence while reducing the perception that any single appointment carries existential political consequences.

Most importantly, however, Americans must restore proper expectations regarding the role of courts themselves.

The judiciary cannot sustainably function as the primary engine for resolving every social, political, and cultural dispute in the country. Similarly, citizens should not look to judges to deliver policy outcomes that the legislative process has seen fit to forego.

That path only deepens polarization and further weakens self-government.

In a healthy constitutional system, courts serve the republic best when they enforce stable rules, protect fundamental rights, and leave the difficult work of policy formation where it belongs — with accountable representatives and the citizens who elect them.

That arrangement will not eliminate disagreement.

But it will help restore a clearer, critical separation between law and politics, a healthier balance between democratic accountability and constitutional restraint, and renewed public confidence that government once again exists to *serve* the people rather than to *manage* them from above.

Because ultimately, the purpose of constitutional government is not to maximize the power of judges, presidents, legislators, or bureaucracies.

It is to preserve the conditions under which free people can pursue fulfilling, happy lives — secure in their liberties and protected from unjust interference by concentrated power, wherever it may emerge.

3. Constitutional Clarity

To some, the very thought of "tinkering" with the Constitution is sacrilegious. To them, it is perfect as is, apparently having sprung from the well of nature, fully formed, exhaustively complete, and entirely relevant and adaptable to all time.

Jefferson disagreed.

Famously, he argued that no generation has the right to bind future generations to its ideas and, therefore, that it only made sense to rewrite our most basic governing charter every 19 years or so.

However, James Madison, the Constitution's principal author, countered that to do so would inject an impractical amount of instability to national affairs and open the door to myriad abuse.

Madison won that argument but, in deference to the undeniable logic and wisdom of Jefferson's point, made sure to include a practical means for amending the document as the changing times might reasonably dictate.

And that is where we stand today, a quarter millennium later.

The Constitution is more than a legal charter.

It is the framework through which Americans understand their rights, their government, and the limits of public power. But most importantly, it's an expression of the nation's foundational purpose:

Protecting the people's freedom to pursue fulfilling, happy lives free from unjust interference.

Its principles remain durable. The structure remains sound. But many of today's political disputes arise not from widespread disagreement over those clearly expressed principles and brilliant structure, but from the uncertainty that comes with converting colonial expression to modern day practice.

It is the ongoing debate between strict constructionism and loose constructionism foreshadowed so long ago by those two brilliant founders.

Over time, constitutional interpretation has shifted from shared understanding toward contested meaning. Phrases written in the eighteenth century are now constantly stretched, twisted, and reinterpreted to fit modern political arguments. As a result, constitutional meaning is often determined less by broad public consensus than by partisan and ideological agendas.

This has consequences beyond academic debate. A healthy system of self-government depends on citizens being able to understand the framework that governs them. When meaning becomes malleable and widely disputed, accountability weakens — not because rights disappear, but because their application becomes increasingly opaque.

A CommonSense approach addresses this directly.

The goal is not to replace founding principles, but to restate them clearly in modern language so they are less dependent on subjective, ever-shifting interpretation and more grounded in shared public understanding.

In practice, this would involve employing Madison's thoughtful amendment process — as has been 27 times to date — and carefully updating constitutional wording so that widely accepted principles are expressed in terms that are unambiguous in contemporary life.

The Second Amendment illustrates the problem clearly. Much of today's conflict does not stem from disagreement over the idea of a right to self-defense or the lawful bearing of arms, but from disputes over historically specific phrasing such as *"well-regulated militia,"* which invites divergent interpretations depending upon one's biased perspective.

This pattern repeats across multiple constitutional provisions. As a result, substantial public energy, time, and resources are wasted on partisan haggling over what we *perceive* those provisions to mean — while never really arriving at an enduring national consensus of what they *actually should* and *do* mean.

Clarification derived from a deliberative, civil, public process would quickly heal such persistently open wounds.

And in addition to clarifying existing language, such a process would also afford us the opportunity to add explicit articulation of rights and protections relating to modern realities that Americans already broadly assume to exist — but which are not expressly addressed.

Personal privacy is another central example.

Americans generally assume strong protections against unreasonable intrusion into their personal lives. But modern surveillance systems, digital communications, artificial intelligence, data collection and sharing, and other emerging technologies pose challenges to privacy the Constitution's framers could not possibly have foreseen. As a result, this fundamental issue is left virtually in its entirety to judges who enforce their wide-ranging perspectives and ideas indirectly through complex layers of politics and interpretation rather than clearly stated constitutional text.

A CommonSense approach would certainly conclude that core constitutional protections — particularly those related to privacy and technological autonomy — should be stated directly and clearly, rather than inferred through evolving judicial doctrine.

This is not about creating new rights. It is about ensuring that existing, widely accepted protections are more broadly and accurately understood and constructed to remain durable in a changed and ever-changing technological environment.

Ongoing neglect of increasingly outdated constitutional language presents great risk, as its continued ambiguity invites perpetual interpretive conflict that steadily erodes public confidence. And that is to say nothing of Jefferson's more philosophical idea challenging our moral right to bind future generations to our values and beliefs.

Effective self-government depends heavily upon clarity of principle and purpose — on shared understanding. And it depends on citizens being able to reasonably comprehend the rules under which they are governed.

Ultimately, constitutional clarity is not a technical exercise. It is a crucial condition of democratic stability —.one which every responsible generation should monitor and attend to ensure continued government fidelity to its most crucial, fundamental purpose.

Because government functions best when ordinary citizens can clearly understand:

what rights they possess,
which powers government holds,
how those powers *must be* restrained,
and the way individual liberty and limited government power work together in service of our shared objective as citizens:

Our free pursuit of fulfilling, happy lives.

PART V: THE WAY FORWARD

1. The Arc of History

Among historians, it is fashionable to look down upon the notion that America was *inevitable.*

In convincing terms, they explain that the independence movement of "ragtag" American patriots could have easily collapsed at multiple moments — that the revolutionary war itself was constantly on the verge of disastrous defeat — and that even in victory, the way forward for America's grand experiment in self-government was anything but assured.

A quarter millennium later, the skeptics are still at it.

Today, anxiety is at a peak over the threat to the "American way of life" — to democracy itself. Pointing to the rise of populism, the decline of democratic institutions and norms, and the death of civility, those same voices that described America as a fragile and curious accident still now stand at this historical intersection holding signs that read, *"The End is Near."*

They were wrong then — they are wrong now.

Not about the inevitability of America's birth between these particular shores — there's nothing magical about this soil.

But they were wrong to doubt the inevitability of the human spirit that drives constantly toward its own progress — toward greater knowledge, greater freedom, and greater capacity for people to control and shape their own lives.

Humanity's timeless and unstoppable *pursuit of happiness.*

Somewhere, somehow, the *idea* of America *was* inevitable — and in 1776, its time had come… here, in the New World.

Today, that pursuit continues for us all. Not in a straight line. Not without setbacks. And certainly not without disagreement or struggle.

In fact, too often we are our own worst enemies. We waste precious energy moving sideways. We set ourselves back years, decades and, at times, even longer by forgetting history's hard-earned lessons and repeating horrific mistakes. We fight each other over trivial, passing interests instead of working together to maximize shared progress on the one that matters most.

We struggle. We sacrifice. We fall. We rise. We fail again — and again.

But still we advance.

We advance by developing and perfecting reliable social structures that provide us with stable, reasonably secure, everyday lives.

We advance by building problem-solving institutions that are resilient and adaptable to constantly changing conditions.

We advance by learning from our explorations and investigations into life's mysteries, hopes, potential, and promise — and by sharing that knowledge with one another.

But the "inevitability" of our advancement does not amount to magic that just happens. Resolving today's challenges and making meaningful progress in our never-ending pursuit of happiness is inevitable because, sooner or later, we *will* do what is required. That is our history — and it's our history because it is our *nature.*

So, the choice before us — the choice *always* before us — is do we act now or do we wait until more dire circumstances finally compel us?

Through every historical moment of human challenge, we have faced that choice — hunker down and wait for the storms to pass, or act with urgency to weatherproof our homes, our communities, and our lives so that we may speed ahead, out from under the rain clouds to continue along a clear path of progress.

We have done both.

But waiting is costly and, therefore, irresponsible. It *delays* the inevitability of progress and ensures for ourselves — and especially for future generations — avoidable hardship. Inherently tasked with maximizing the happiness of our time on earth while ensuring the same opportunity for our children, waiting to solve problems and overcome challenges that will not go away on their own is the ultimate act of human negligence.

And it is the hidden cost of America's political dysfunction.

Because time lost to needless delay is not worthless. It is paid for somewhere — by families, by communities, and by the next generation, who inherit problems they did not create and are asked to solve them under the same inherited broken conditions.

Our obligation to the next generation is simple but serious: leave society in at least as good a condition as we found it, persistently striving to ensure that they are not forced to relive the same debates, the same failures, and the same avoidable conflicts and hardships.

That does not require perfection. It requires effort. Determined, inexhaustible, relentless effort.

It requires refusing to accept unnecessary breakdowns as permanent.

It requires rejecting the idea that dysfunction is simply "the way it is."

And it requires resisting the justification that *they* will surely fix what *we* choose to neglect.

This is the real weight of civic responsibility in a free society.

More than just going through the motions of participating in elections or debates and telling ourselves we tried — but doing the persistent work of keeping our society focused on its fundamental purpose, holding our leaders accountable to that purpose, and ensuring that the America we pass forward is better than the one passed to us.

When people believe that positive change is outside their control, they stop trying to make it. And when that belief becomes widespread, progress slows — not because solutions do not exist, but because the will to pursue them has been lost, even if only temporarily.

The challenge, then, is to not *rest* in the comfort that progress will eventually come — but to *minimize* the periodic and costly delays along the way.

America will eventually, *inevitably* continue along humanity's historical arc of progress. But will we act decisively *now* to end our present detour and get back on track — as we have in the past — or will we wait and allow the cost to accrue until we finally decide our problems can no longer be ignored?

2. We the People

Understanding how "the system" works is not an academic exercise.

It changes how we see things and how we act — how *We the People* act.

Once we realize that the self-governing choices we are repeatedly presented are artificially incomplete — that they are framed too narrowly and often exclude practical, more appealing alternatives — it becomes harder to accept them.

Once we recognize how responsibility is constantly shifted, blurred, or altogether denied in ways that prevent accountability, it becomes harder to ignore.

And once we remember how ordinary people just like us — at crucial moments throughout human history — have repeatedly overcome the "unrealistic" to return again and again to the irresistible pursuit of fulfilling, happy lives, it becomes harder to avoid a simple question:

What are we waiting for?

That question is the beginning of real change.

No slogans.
No sides.
No shouting matches inside the same broken system.

Just everyday citizens deciding that they are no longer willing to accept the way things are simply because it's the way things are.

What follows from that awakening — as it has in all of those historically crucial moments — is *reclamation.*

Not constant political engagement. Not turning everyday life into a *defeats-the-purpose* kind of political obsession. But a conscious return to the basic responsibilities of self-government: paying attention, asking better questions, and enforcing clear accountability for decisions affecting communities and families.

Government is not something that *happens* to people.

It's a force *we impose upon ourselves* — one we can either control or allow to control us.

Time and again, history has shown us our nature to let control slip from our hands into those of a trusted few, granting ourselves the freedom to focus more of our energy and effort on daily life. It is entirely understandable.

But it has also shown us how that shift gradually results in an untenable imbalance — at first barely noticeable, soon thereafter concerning and then, eventually, intolerably dangerous.

Most importantly, however, it has shown us our ability to reclaim that control in sheer defiance of our own self-limiting belief that it couldn't be done.

Because *we have done it* — over and over and over again, we've managed to break free of Radical Realism's grasp long enough to do what we had insisted to ourselves was impossible.

Surely by now *we must know that we can.*

And yet, our discontent continues to grow.

We're not happy with the way things are.

We are deeply dissatisfied with the options we are constantly offered as alternatives.

We have become convinced that we are powerless to enforce accountability that leads to meaningful change.

And we have come to believe that anything outside the False Choice Paradigm is "unrealistic."

Like facts to Adams, however, self-evident truths are stubborn things — and down deep we know them well enough to make all the difference.

We know that a naturally occurring Corrupt Power Establishment has engineered politics and government to serve the interests of the few at the expense of the many.

We know that UnCompromising Extremism is responsible for perpetual conflict and widespread exhaustion.

We know CommonSense Americans comprise an overwhelming majority that desperately desires meaningful change.

And we know that in past times of desperation, this CommonSense Majority has risen above Radical Realism to accomplish extraordinary things.

We *know* all of this and still we wait.

For *what*?

For better leaders?

For better circumstances?

For better… *luck*?

Or are we really just postponing necessary reform until frustration deepens into true national crisis and *forces* us into action — secretly hoping that that time won't come until we're gone and it's the next generation's problem to solve?

Because another self-evident truth appears to be that, for all our complaining, things clearly haven't reached a tipping point of intolerability. Apparently, our problems aren't as daunting as the prospect of exerting the effort required to solve them.

But we also now understand that waiting for our circumstances to reach the bottom — when it's clear that's the direction they're heading — is an act of utmost neglect. Because it forfeits the opportunity for meaningful correction under relatively peaceful, practical, and manageable conditions while, again, posing the risk of avoidable hardship to future generations.

So, is now the time that those future generations may look back upon as the moment we finally broke history's pattern of costly procrastination and acted with responsible haste to minimize their hardships?

Or will it simply be one more sideways datapoint of wasted time, energy, and resources on the graph that otherwise illustrates a long arc of progress?

Real change does not begin in Washington.

It begins when ordinary citizens stop accepting the conditioned belief that they are powerless to influence what happens there.

The CommonSense Majority does not lack numbers.
It does not lack intelligence.
It does not lack practical instincts or shared motivation.

What it lacks is organization, focus, and inspirational leadership capable of overcoming the negative incentives that currently dominate political life.

That is why reclaiming control must begin with accountability — consistent accountability applied by We the People equally to everyone who contributes to dysfunction, division, corruption, or institutional irresponsibility.

That accountability neither starts nor ends at the ballot box.

It starts with the clear expression of demands for structural reforms that will loosen extremists' control over elections and return genuine competitiveness to the political system itself. Party-engineered "safe" districts, partisan primaries, and electoral systems designed to protect incumbents have insulated government from meaningful public correction for far too long.

But merely "demanding" reform — as we have far too often seen — will not be enough. Our efforts must continue by bringing real pressure to bear — the kind that forces politicians to hear and act upon those demands — in simple, smart, strategically targeted ways.

This we can and must do.

Because if all we do is shout our CommonSense demands into the wind, nothing will change and that failure will only further reinforce our debilitating sense of powerlessness.

And while the necessary effort to maintain and exercise responsible control over our self-government can never really end, the process of *reclaiming* it will only conclude when — as explained here previously — we demonstrate once and for all to ambitious politicians that the fate of their careers lies in *our* hands and not those of Uncompromising Extremists.

A government that cannot be held accountable cannot remain responsive for long.

And a political system that rewards conflict more than competence will continue producing exactly the kind of leadership Americans abhor.

Fortunately, these problems are not beyond our ability to solve — history makes that much clear.

Reclaiming control of our self-government does not require turning politics into an everyday obsession.

It requires something far simpler — *simple but not easy*: citizens who are willing to pay attention, reject manipulation, think independently, demand practical reform, and consistently enforce accountability from those entrusted with public power.

That's when government will once again answer to We the People — the CommonSense Majority — and return its focus to better supporting our ongoing pursuit of fulfilling and happy everyday lives.

Conclusion

Too often we confuse complexity for intelligence — and, conversely, simplicity for naivete.

The perverse result is that we trust the people and ideas we understand least, while dismissing out of hand those that make the most sense and most closely reflect our own instincts, experiences, and true desires.

Jefferson, Madison, and the other founders understood that well — and they didn't allow their simple but revolutionary objective to be derailed by pointless complication. And to their credit, the everyday citizens of those 13 tiny, diverse colonies listened and understood the power of the self-evident truths that demanded "liberty or death" as the simple terms of their struggle for independence.

Because the central truth underlying our American experiment is actually quite straight forward:

Most of us want the same basic thing — something that is not partisan, not extreme, and certainly not naive.

Something as timelessly human as it gets.

We may express it in countless different ways, but each of those expressions is nothing more than another way of saying the same thing.

And it bears repeating — again and again.

America and its self-government exists for one reason and one reason only — to support its people's ongoing pursuit of fulfilling, happy everyday lives, free from excessive and unjust interference.

Over time, however, America's political and institutional incentives have steadily drifted away from that purpose and become distorted in service to the few at the expense of the many.

A naturally occurring Corrupt Power Establishment benefits from confusion, division, and perpetual conflict among everyday folks — so it is incentivized to maintain and reinforce the status quo.

UnCompromising Extremists who comprise a tiny fraction of us increasingly dominate political life by convincing those same folks that every disagreement is existential and every election a battle for national survival — so they are incentivized to keep us angry, afraid, and enslaved to the False Choice Paradigm.

And Radical Realists have been conditioned to believe that positive change is impossible and that only fools would waste their time, energy, and money chasing it — so they are incentivized to ignore efforts to achieve it while resigning themselves to the notion that the *lesser evil* is their only "realistic" option.

The result is an exhausted and discouraged public that has forgotten its own power.

CommonSense Americans are pressured to believe that somehow *we* are the minority — too scattered, too unsophisticated, too *powerless* to reclaim meaningful control over *our* government and redirect it toward its proper purpose.

And we buy it.

But history tells us something very different.

Again and again, everyday people have risen to overcome conditions once widely accepted as permanent or inescapable and put themselves back on track to greater happiness. America's own revolution — when the Radical Realists of that time insisted that defeating the mighty British was impossible — is but one example.

That suggests that progress *is* inevitable — not because it emerges magically on its own, but because human beings eventually refuse to continue tolerating conditions that stand too long in the way of their pursuit of better lives.

Eventually, they choose to act. Every time.

The question, therefore, is not whether Americans possess the ability to correct our present course.

We clearly do.

Rather, it is whether we will act *before* unnecessary hardship *forces* us to.

Because the hidden cost of political dysfunction is not merely frustration in the present. It is wasted time. Delayed progress. Preventable hardship unnecessarily passed forward to future generations while we postpone changes that deep down we *know* to be both essential and achievable.

CommonSense tells us we should not wait.

We already possess the numbers.

We already possess the shared interests and practical instincts.

And we already possess the power necessary to restore accountability, rebalance authority, and redirect government back toward its fundamental purpose — *our* fundamental purpose.

In fact, in many respects, America's history is a real life never ending story of generational devotion to timeless causes like liberty, justice, equality, and opportunity — all of which add up to the pursuit of that purpose.

And so it must also be asked — what will be *our* contribution to that story?

Will it be the important but superficial advancement of technological achievement and new invention?

Or will it be a renewed commitment to something even more fundamental — the thing that actually drives those advancements — the thing that those advancements themselves are meant to serve but which has become detached and lost along the way: the pursuit of genuinely fulfilling and happier lives for *all of us.*

We can — we *must* recover our confidence and rededicate ourselves to government *of* the people, *by* the people, and *for* the people.

Not because the work is easy.

Not because success is guaranteed.

But because it is our solemn obligation to ourselves and our posterity.

That idea has not failed. It has only been forgotten — and what has been forgotten can be restored.

Perhaps not all at once.

Certainly not without effort.

But deliberately, responsibly, and peacefully by citizens who remember their own inherent strength, reject conditioned resignation, reclaim control, and reassert meaningful accountability.

Sooner or later, the CommonSense Majority *will* rise to do exactly that.

We should stop waiting and do it *now*.

About the Author

James Peppe is a political scientist, executive leader, strategic advisor, and civic advocate whose career has spanned politics, government, business, and public affairs.

A graduate of Yale University, Peppe has spent decades working at the intersection of public policy and organizational leadership, advising elected officials, political campaigns, advocacy organizations, senior executives, and institutions navigating complex challenges. His experience includes leadership roles in government affairs, financial services, and association management, as well as extensive involvement in political strategy and citizen engagement.

In 2020, Peppe sought the Republican nomination for President of the United States, motivated by growing concern over political extremism, civic disengagement, and the increasing inability of America's political system to advance practical solutions. That experience reinforced his conviction that the nation's greatest challenges are not primarily ideological, but structural—and that meaningful reform remains both possible and necessary.

He is the creator and host of *PepTalks with James Peppe*, a video podcast dedicated to helping everyday Americans better understand politics, government, and their own power within the system. He is also the founder of *Pursuit America*, a nonprofit civic initiative focused on empowering the CommonSense Majority and restoring government's fundamental purpose: supporting the freedom of Americans to pursue fulfilling, happy lives.

To learn more about the author and his related works, visit:

jamespeppe.carrd.co

Made in the USA
Coppell, TX
21 June 2026

83110480R00049